FANNIE NEVER FLINCHED

ONE WOMAN'S COURAGE IN THE STRUGGLE FOR AMERICAN LABOR UNION RIGHTS

MARY CRONK FARRELL

ABRAMS BOOKS FOR YOUNG READERS · NEW YORK

Library of Congress Cataloging-in-Publication Data
Farrell, Mary Cronk.
Fannie never flinched : one woman's courage in the struggle for
American labor union rights / Mary Cronk Farrell.
pages cm
ISBN 978-1-4197-1884-7 (hardcover)
1. Sellins, Fannie, 1872–1919—Juvenile literature. 2. Women labor
leaders—United States—Biography—Juvenile literature.
3. Labor unions—Organizing—United States—History—Juvenile
literature. 4. Labor unions—United States—History—Juvenile
literature. I. Title.
HD6509.S45 F37 2016
331.88092—dc23
2015040020

Printed and bound in China
10 9 8 7 6 5 4 3 2 1

Abrams Books for Young Readers are available at special discounts
when purchased in quantity for premiums and promotions as well as
fund-raising or educational use. Special editions can also be created
to specification. For details, contact specialsales@abramsbooks.com
or the address below.

115 West 18th Street
New York, NY 10011
www.abramsbooks.com

IMAGE CREDITS

Title page: Special Collections Library, Fred Waring's America, Penn State University Libraries. **Opposite page 1:** Special Collections Library, Fred Waring's America, Penn State University Libraries. **Page 3:** Brown Brothers Photography. **Page 4:** Kheel Center for Labor-Management Documentation & Archives, Cornell University, Collection: International Ladies Garment Workers Union Photographs (1885-1985). **Page 5 (top):** Kheel Center for Labor-Management Documentation & Archives, Cornell University, Collection: International Ladies Garment Workers Union Photographs (1885-1985). **Page 5 (bottom):** *Shelter and Clothing* by Helen Kinne (New York: The Macmillan Company, 1920), 202. **Page 7 (left):** From the Albert R. Stone Negative Collection, Rochester Museum & Science Center, Rochester, NY. **Page 7 (above):** DN-005632 Chicago Daily News Negatives Collection, Chicago History Museum. **Page 8:** Missouri History Museum, St. Louis. **Page 9:** National Archives and Records. **Page 10:** Library of Congress. **Page 11 (above):** *The News Tribune*, Tacoma, Washington. **Page 11 (right):** The Portland Labor Press. **Page 13 (left):** Library of Congress. **Page 13 (below):** West Virginia & Regional History Collection, UVW Libraries. **Page 14:** Denver Public Library, Western History Collection #X-60388. **Page 15 (left):** West Virginia & Regional History Collection, UVW Libraries. **Page 15 (below):** Denver Public Library, Western History Collection #X60448. **Page 16:** National Archives and Records. **Page 17:** National Archives and Records. **Page 18:** Library of Congress. **Page 19 (above):** Carnegie Mellon University Archives. **Page 19 (right):** Robin G. Lighty Collection. **Page 20:** Courtesy of Janet Lindenmuth. **Page 21:** University of Pittsburgh. **Page 24:** Grandville Heights/Marble Cliff Historical Society, Columbus, Ohio. **Page 25:** National Archives and Records. **Page 27 (both left and below):** National Archives and Records. **Page 28:** *The New York Times*. **Page 29 (left):** Courtesy of Anthony Slomkowski. **Page 29 (below):** University of Pittsburgh. **Page 30:** Special Collections Library, Fred Waring's America, Penn State University Libraries. **Page 31:** Author's collection. **Page 33:** West Virginia and Regional History Collection, UVW Libraries. **Page 37:** Denver Public Library, Western History Collection #Z 199. **Page 38:** National Archives, Records of the U.S. Information Agency (306-NT-94692). **Page 39:** Kenneth Rogers Collection, Atlanta History Center, Atlanta, GA.

CONTENTS

A STORM CENTER FOR BULLETS

NATRONA, PENNSYLVANIA, AUGUST 26, 1919

Near suppertime, gunshots echoed among the small frame houses of Natrona, Pennsylvania. People ran out to see what was happening. Seven-year-old Stanley F. Rafalko was on his way to the corner store to get his father a packet of cigarettes. When he came out, he saw sheriff's deputies beating a man with blackjacks, and shooting over the heads of a crowd of women and children.

Dozens of witnesses say a woman named Fannie Sellins herded a group of children toward safety behind the Rafalko family's backyard gate.

"Stop, before someone gets hurt!" Fannie shouted at the deputies.

The officers turned their weapons on her.

"Stop!" she shouted again.

The local newspaper would later report she appeared to be a "storm center" for deputies' bullets.

OPPOSITE Young eyewitnesses to the fatal shooting of Fannie Sellins, including Stanley F. Rafalko (third from right). Brackenridge, Pennsylvania, August 1919.

1

FANNIE STITCHES TOGETHER A DREAM

St. Louis, Missouri, 1897

Fannie's head pounded from the racket of the high-speed sewing machines. Dozens of mechanized needles pumping up and down sounded a continuous *clickety-clack, clickety-clack* over the rumble of foot treadles and the whir of spinning spools of thread.

"Faster!" the boss shouted. "Work faster!"

Fannie longed to stretch her arms and legs and straighten her back, but she kept a firm hand on the fabric, feeding it steadily under the needle. One stray glance and the needle could tear through her finger. It happened once or twice a day to some girl in the factory.

"You bleed on the fabric, you pay for it," the boss always said.

Fannie worked at one of two sweatshops owned and operated by the Marx & Haas Clothing Co., the largest clothing manufacturer in St. Louis. She sewed silk-lined hunting coats, each with eleven pockets. Finishing a pocket, Fannie rubbed her bleary eyes and moved on to the next.

Fannie Mooney Sellins was born in 1867, the oldest daughter of an Irish family living in

2

Women and girls at a factory similar to the one where Fannie worked pause their sewing machines for a photograph. Notice the male supervisor standing behind the workers. New York, c. 1910.

Cincinnati, Ohio. Her father worked as a house-painter, and her mother worked at home caring for the family. Fannie had one older brother, a younger sister, and three younger brothers. In the 1870s, the Mooneys moved to St. Louis, Missouri, where Fannie went to school, learned to read and write, and finished the eighth grade.

She eventually married Charles Sellins and they had four children. Charles died when the youngest was still a baby. To support her family, Fannie went to work at the garment factory. Coughing from the sweatshop's foul air, Fannie

Rose Schneiderman, like Fannie, a garment worker and union organizer, works next to the large pile of fabric that makes up her day's assignment. New York City, 1908.

dropped the presser foot onto a new seam. Most young seamstresses working with her at the garment factory in St. Louis never had the chance to go to school. Girls as young as ten and women old enough to be grandmothers labored alongside her. They worked ten- to fourteen-hour days, six days a week. The building was hot and stifling in the summer—and bitter cold in the winter.

"All the doors were locked from the outside at 7:15 each morning. Sometimes it made me sick to think what would happen in that big flimsy barracks if a fire should come," Fannie said.

The families of most of the seamstresses had immigrated from country villages in Italy, Poland, and Russia, just as the Irish had come fifty years before, hoping for a better life in America.

Though poor and unable to read or write, they knew how to work hard, which was exactly what garment manufacturers in St. Louis wanted. Like Fannie, the new immigrants barely earned enough to live on, averaging less than five dollars a week ($145 today). If anyone complained, the boss could fire them. There were always immigrants desperate for jobs.

Fannie heard seamstresses in Chicago and New York City had banded together and demanded higher pay and safer working conditions. They had joined a union, the United Garment Workers of America, or the UGWA.

Toiling at her sewing machine, Fannie stitched together a dream. If women and girls in other cities could organize a union to improve their jobs, those in St. Louis could, too! During brief lunch breaks, she spoke with her co-workers. "If we earned a fair wage, your children wouldn't have to work," she said. "They could go to school."

Uniting forces would give workers more clout to bargain with their employers. If they didn't get fair wages and safe working conditions, they could strike. In a strike, workers walked off the job and refused to go back until the company agreed to their demands. If all the workers stuck together and didn't give in, the factory had to shut down, and the company owners lost money. Unions gave workers the power to bargain with employers and improve their lives.

In 1902, Fannie and the other seamstresses launched Ladies' Local 67 of the United Garment Workers of America. Marx & Haas managers feared that the new union would strike. They agreed to nearly double the workers' wages and shorten the workday.

TOP An immigrant family carrying their possessions as they arrive on a ship to America, c. 1900. Location unknown.

BOTTOM The United Garment Workers of America (UGWA) label affixed inside clothing. Some tags bore background text such as *Special Order* or *Duck Goods*. Duck was the type of fabric Fannie made into coats.

FANNIE FINDS HER VOICE

1909–1910

Fannie managed to earn enough to feed her children and send them to school, but she never made enough money to escape poverty.

Despite Marx & Haas Clothing Company's concessions to the labor union, the workrooms were crowded and the air was filthy. Many of the employees got sick with tuberculosis, a highly contagious, incurable disease that often became fatal. If they arrived to work even a few minutes late, as punishment they were locked in the basement for an hour and not allowed to go to their sewing machines. Because seamstresses were paid by the number of garments they sewed each day, the lost hour was precious.

Company owners seemed to be on the lookout for a chance to challenge and ultimately break the garment workers' union. In 1909 they found one. A man who worked as a tailor at Marx & Haas tried to use the elevator instead of walking up six flights of stairs to the workroom floor. He had trouble breathing because he suffered from tuberculosis. Although the boss had ordered the tailor to take the stairs, he refused. The boss docked him a

week's pay. To protest this unfairness, Fannie and many union workers walked out of the factory.

The next day, September 13, 1909, Marx & Haas locked out all one thousand union workers and gave their jobs to nonunion people. Fannie organized strikers to march in a picket line in front of the factory. They carried protest signs and tried to convince the replacement workers not to take their jobs.

"Not fair!" they shouted. "Scabs!"

Union members used the word *scab* for strikebreakers, people willing to cross the picket line

LEFT After an eight-week strike, the United Garment Workers of America (largely women and children) and the Clothiers Exchange agreed on abolition of subcontractors, a fifty-two-hour workweek, time and a half for overtime, no work on five legal holidays, and no discrimination for strike activity. Rochester, New York, 1913.

ABOVE Police arrest a woman for picketing during a garment workers' strike in Chicago, similar to Fannie's strike in St. Louis. Eventually, 41,000 garment workers join the walkout. Chicago, Illinois, 1910.

and work during a strike. It was an insult, as if calling someone lousy or rotten.

So many workers refused to cross the picket line, the plant nearly had to close. Marx & Haas went to court to stop the picketing. The judge agreed with the company owners and told strik-

ers that they must stop protesting and return to the factory, or they would lose their jobs. Fannie and other union leaders would be arrested if they even walked down the street by the Marx & Haas building! The workers stopped picketing, but did not go back to work. The strike continued.

One month into the labor dispute, UGWA Local 67's president died of tuberculosis, and Fannie became president. Her youngest daughter was now twelve, and Fannie agreed to work for the UGWA full-time. She traveled from city to city, telling people about the low wages and unhealthy working conditions at Marx & Haas, and asking them to support the striking garment workers.

At first, Fannie was scared when she stood onstage to speak to a crowd, but remembering the anxious faces of the hardworking girls at their sewing machines gave her strength and courage.

"Help us fight," she told union coal miners during a speech in Illinois in November 1909. "We women work in factories on dangerous machinery, and many of us get horribly injured or killed. Many of your brothers die in the mines. There

should be a bond of sympathy between us, for we both encounter danger in our daily work."

The miners stomped their feet and shouted their agreement. Some were so moved by Fannie's speech, they wiped tears from their eyes.

Traveling the country for two years, Fannie saw workers everywhere had the same troubles: long hours, low pay, and dangerous conditions.

In December 1909, Fannie visited Chicago, where she discovered that girls in button facto-

ries worked in unheated buildings, and often cut their fingers on jagged mussel shells. A cut might not seem serious, but continually reaching into tubs of dirty water for the shells, the girls risked fatal infection. At the time, there were more cases of pneumonia, typhus, and gangrene among button factory laborers than in any other industry.

In Detroit cigar factories, ten-year-old boys had to stand on benches in order to reach their work. With fingers stained from tobacco, they

OPPOSITE Women and girls sewing in a clothing shop, likely a smaller operation than the garment factory where Fannie worked. Speedy sewing was essential, as like Fannie, they did piecework, meaning they were paid per piece of finished clothing. St. Louis, Missouri, date unknown.

ABOVE Coal miners take a break. The boy, Joseph "Jo" Puma (seated), worked as a nipper, fetching and carrying for the miners and learning the trade. Jo's mother said he was fourteen years old. Pittston, Pennsylvania, January 1911.

tied wet sponges over their nostrils to block out poisonous fumes.

Traveling for months, Fannie spoke at union halls across the country. She asked people to sup-

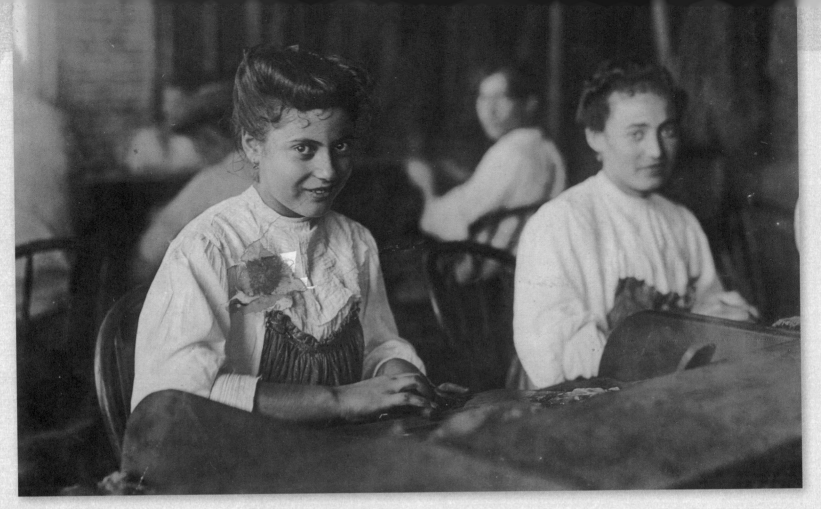

Factory owners viewed young girls and boys as well-suited to making cigars due to their small hands. Children were also more manageable, cheaper, and less likely to strike than adult workers. The youngsters first cut the cigar wrappers to their proper length with a sharp, handleless chaveta knife, then measured and formed the tobacco into bundles, which they placed in the wrappers, using a special board to finally roll and seal the cigar. Tampa, Florida, 1909.

port the striking garment workers in St. Louis by buying only clothes with the "union-made" label inside them. Those tags guaranteed that the workers who made those garments were treated better. Shirts and trousers without the union label came from sweatshops like the one where Fannie had worked.

In July 1910, Fannie spoke to union carpenters in Iowa. Her voice rang with feeling and her dark eyes snapped. "Injury to one is an injury to all!" she said. People jumped to their feet, clapping and whooping so hard, the ruckus nearly shook the building.

"Pass the hat!" someone hollered, and a cap

Two Women Fighting Sweatshop System to Help Save Bodies and Souls of Children

ST. LOUIS, Oct. 16.—Here are two women, Catherine Hurley and Fannie Sellins, who are making a successful fight for better working conditions for the women and children in the sweat shops.

Bitter experience in a St. Louis sweat shop where they worked 13 and 14 hours a day drove them into the fight.

"In those days — before we formed the union that enforced the nine-hour day, the shop was open at 7:15; and if you weren't there on time you didn't get in," said Miss Sellins.

"All the doors were locked at 7:15. Sometimes it made me sick to think what would happen in that big flimsy barracks if a fire should come.

"We had half an hour off at noon to eat, an hour off between 5 and 6, and then the whole crowd, children of 10 and 11 and old women with the rest, worked until 9. The kids made $1 or so a week, and no one more than $6. Well, the union changed that.

"But change the children's wages? We were never able to help those babies. There's a terrible system in St. Louis. They politely call it the 'permit system.' A child, no matter its age, can go to the city hall and by merely stating that its wage is necessary to help support the family can get a permit.

"The state of Missouri is all that can help them. And the state doesn't care."

CATHERINE HURLEY   FANNIE SELLINS

Women In the News

Omitting the Word "Obey" Makes Marriages Happy, Court Says.

Omitting the word "obey" from the ceremony has a tendency to promote happy marriages, accord—

riage so vigorously at Washingt[on] that she announced she wou[ld] leave her home and never co[me] back if he wed Sarah Wetzel, Clarendon, Va.

ABOVE A story in the *Tacoma Times* tells of Fannie's work, dateline: "St. Louis, Missouri, October 16, 1911."

RIGHT A newspaper advertisement showing various union labels, and urging consumers to demand that products they buy carry the label, thus promoting better wages and working conditions for laborers.

Demand The Label

It is the cheapest and most effective way to secure better conditions for the toilers.

The great army of wage earners—as represented in the labor movement of this country—with its enormous factory output of $20,000,000,000, by continually advocating the use of the label, is doing more to make this world a better place to live in than all the other organizations combined.

Insist On Having These Labels

went hand to hand. Coins jingled and bills rustled. The union carpenters donated one thousand dollars ($25,700 today) to help the striking garment workers in St. Louis feed their families.

Fannie spoke as many as six times a day, and people listened. So many refused to buy non-

union clothing that Marx & Haas had to close one factory. With the money Fannie raised, the St. Louis strikers held out for two years until Marx & Haas gave in to the union. Working conditions did not substantially improve, but the company agreed to re-hire union workers and raise wages.

ANGEL OF MERCY

News of Fannie's leadership in the garment workers' union reached coal miners in Colliers, West Virginia, and she was asked to visit.

Fannie found miners' families in rickety houses with no running water. They lived on biscuits and boiled beans, maybe a little bacon. Children fell asleep to the sound of their bellies growling.

The men worked sunup to sundown like Fannie had in the garment factory, but they went underground with picks and shovels. Sometimes damp and cold, sometimes stooped over or kneeling, but always covered in coal-black grime.

Boys started in the mine as early as age six or seven. Some "nippers" crawled into crannies to chip away the coal. Other little boys sat long hours fighting to stay awake in complete darkness. Their job was to fling open the heavy wooden doors for the mules hauling ore through the tunnels to daylight.

In Colliers, Fannie saw the bony-legged children and their mothers' empty eyes, and she realized that her dream of better lives for all workers was a long way off. Still, she didn't give up—she got busy.

Striking was the only way workers could try to influence the mine owners, but Fannie knew that the miners would not stay on strike if their children were hungry. She solicited donations of

LEFT Mules stabled deep underground pulled carts loaded with coal out of the mines. Young mule drivers worked from 7:00 a.m. to 5:30 p.m. Mine owners considered the mules more valuable than the human workers. Workers could be replaced easily, but mules cost money. Brown Mine, West Virginia, September 1908.

BELOW Coal miners' children play in front of company housing. Grant Town, West Virginia, c. 1915.

The United Mine Workers Union raised funds from members across the country to provide food and sheltzer for workers on strike like these in Ludlow, Colorado, 1914.

food and clothing for the miners' families. Her charisma and passion roused the workers, as she cared for the sick and helped mothers in childbirth. Union families called her an angel of mercy.

The miners whispered about organizing a union, and Fannie encouraged them, but a judge had outlawed the United Mine Workers of America, or UMWA, in the region. Men could be fired for even talking about it!

Union followers held secret meetings.

"Might as well starve striking than working," some said.

But others argued, "Too risky."

The coal company owned them body and soul. It owned the shanties they lived in, the stores where they bought groceries, and even the schools and churches.

The day finally came when each man had to decide for himself. Union leaders marched to the mouth of the Colliers mine with a brass band. As miners came off shift, the union signed up those willing to strike.

But mine managers refused to acknowledge that the miners had the right to join a labor union. They evicted families from their houses, dumping everything they owned on the ground. Bosses hauled in a trainload of strikebreakers to replace the workers. And a federal judge threatened to arrest anyone who spoke in support of the union, whether "in their homes or on the streets."

The antiunion coalfields of West Virginia came close to the feudal systems of the Middle Ages, where the lower classes worked for landowners and remained indebted to them for life. Fannie's attempts to organize mine workers and

give comfort to their families was called "inciting to riot" by the local authorities. Most of what Fannie was doing at the time would be called social work today.

December 3, 1913, Fannie joined the striking miners in a huge rally to show solidarity. She knew if she spoke out for her dream, she might go to jail. She climbed right up onto the platform.

"I am free and I have a right to walk or talk any place in this country as long as I obey the law," she said. Miners whistled and shouted. Women and children cheered.

"The only wrong I have done is to take shoes to the children in Colliers whose bare feet are blue from the cruel blasts of winter," Fannie said. "If it's wrong to put shoes on those little feet, then I will continue to do wrong as long as I have hands and feet to crawl to Colliers."

Fannie was arrested for defying the antiunion injunction, but the judge let her off with a warning. She stuck with the striking union families through the winter.

They lived in tents, depending on the kindness of others for food and clothing. The women and children sometimes heard gunfire as company guards took strikebreakers to the mine each day and strikers tried to stop them. One guard was wounded, one striker killed.

Still, Fannie never stopped believing in her dream. She inspired the women around her to dream, too. When the miners wondered if they should quit the strike, their wives told them to hang tough.

One spring day in April 1914, as nonunion workers neared the mine, a striker threw a punch, and everybody jumped in slugging. With knuckles and clubs, the union men chased the strikebreakers from the mine to the railroad depot and put them on the next train out of town.

Eleven men were accused of being ringleaders in the fracas and arrested. Fannie took no part in the fight, but she was arrested, too. "I do not advise violence," Fannie said. "Except in self-defense as a last resort."

Union lawyers argued to free Fannie and the men, but they lost the case. Fannie was sentenced to six months in jail, and the union did not have enough money to post her bail. Union members photographed her behind bars and put the picture on postcards. People from all over the country sent the postcards to President Woodrow Wilson, asking him to free Fannie.

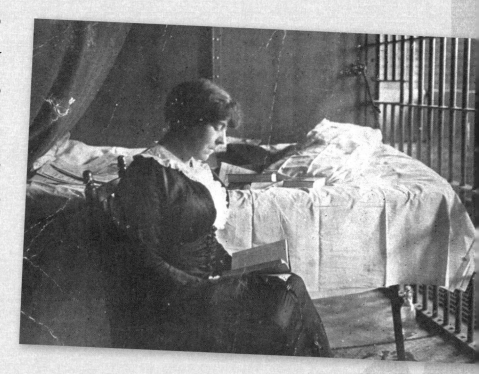

POST CARD

Your Excellency:

I herewith respectfully petition you to release Fannie Sellins, at present confined in the Marion County Jail, Fairmont, W. Va., under a six months sentence inflicted by Judge A. G. Dayton.

She is not charged with the violation of any law of the state or nation, but with the alleged violation of Judge Dayton's own injunction, which has been appealed. She is the only woman in a jail containing no provisions for women, and this makes her imprisonment simply torture.

(Signed) ....

(Address) ....

PUT ONE CENT STAMP HERE

Hon. Woodrow Wilson,

President of the United States,

WASHINGTON, D. C.

36

Living with the poor miners' families, Fannie had become weak from working so hard and not eating enough. In jail, her health grew worse. The Marion County jail had no sanitary facilities for women. In her cell, Fannie was in view of any men who might walk by, some of whom were drunk and disorderly. The jail cells were constructed in tiers three high, and Fannie's cell was on the top tier where men below could peer up at her through a grating. The jail physician wrote the Marion County Board of Health that due to "close confinement and very hot weather" Fannie risked great injury to her health.

The coal company and the strikers finally reached an agreement. Miners would get a raise in pay, but the union would have to go. Mine owners refused to deal with the UMWA. The union raised enough money to free Fannie after she had served three months. Later, President Wilson pardoned her and several other union organizers.

After her stretch in jail, most folks would not have blamed Fannie if she gave up fighting for poor workers. But Fannie could not stand by and do nothing. In her mind, it was a matter of justice.

LABOR WAR

Across the West Virginia state line, in Pennsylvania's Alle-Kiski Valley, known as Black Valley, some of the richest corporations in America piled up profits. Their owners, such as J. P. Morgan and Andrew Carnegie, wore diamonds, while their workers wore rags.

Again, Fannie's fiery words reminded workers that they deserved better. In a wave of strikes in Western Pennsylvania, box makers, steelworkers, laundrywomen, and machinists all won higher pay.

Still, coal miners in the Allegheny and Kiskiminetas river valleys, a region rich with natural resources, seemed stuck in poverty. Natrona sat on the western bluff of the Allegheny River north-

Business tycoon John Pierpont "J. P." Morgan's daughter (center) and friends frequented the Coaching Club of New York to enjoy polo, horse racing, and tennis. Date unknown.

ABOVE Andrew Carnegie's main residence was a
mansion on Fifth Avenue in New York City. Here,
he's pictured at his golf cottage. Westchester
County, New York, 1911.

RIGHT Children standing in the dirt street of
a company coal town, showing typical houses
with a mine shaft in the background. Western
Pennsylvania, c. 1910.

east of Pittsburgh. The town bustled with Italian, Polish, and Slavic immigrant families who raised flocks of ducks and geese on the river much as they had in the Old Country. Wealthier native-born Americans in Allegheny County gave the place the derogatory name Ducktown. They were suspicious of the foreigners, who didn't speak English, ate strange foods, and had strange customs.

Despite prejudice, the immigrants exhibited a pioneering spirit, building ethnic churches, grocery stores, and fraternal halls. But their well-tended vegetable gardens, small frame houses, and privies were blackened with soot from coal-burning steel plants nearby. Families couldn't seem to get ahead. Fathers and sons followed paths down the bluff to the nearby coal mines in Brackenridge, where they worked twelve hours a day, six days a week. On payday near the entrances to the mines, lines of maimed and debilitated workers begged for handouts.

Pennsylvania coal country was the most dangerous place to work in America. Death and injury waited in the dark shafts where rock fractured and crashed down without warning. On average, a man died in the mines every day, often crushed by coal cars or killed by explosions.

When children heard the whistle blow, they stopped playing and ran home. They waited with their mothers, hearts pounding, as men came up the street carrying the limp body. Covered with coal dust, miners' faces all looked alike. At which house would the silent procession stop? Sooner or later, nearly every family lost a father, brother, or son.

But that's not why union people called it Black Valley. The dismal name came from the bleak opportunities workers faced in the region, where iron, coal, and steel companies had busted unions for two decades. Fighting between labor unions and mine owners was so fierce, they called it war. Labor War.

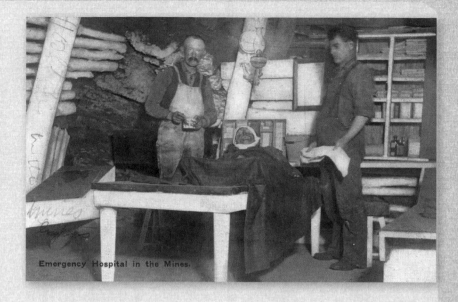

Emergency Hospital in the Mines.

ABOVE An injured miner receives treatment at the emergency hospital at a Pennsylvania mine. Date unknown.

OPPOSITE Pennsylvania's mounted Coal and Iron Police were so notoriously brutal, miners nicknamed them Cossacks. In Russia, Cossack soldiers hired by the czars massacred people and burned villages to put down peasant uprisings and destroy Jewish communities.

A millionaire named Lewis Hicks ran fourteen mines where bosses treated workers like slaves. He paid less than other companies did, made his miners work two hours a day longer, and cared little if miners got hurt on the job.

Every day Fannie talked to Black Valley miners and their families, telling the women they deserved to live like Americans: have bathtubs, indoor plumbing, and sanitary homes with cur-

tains on the windows. Their children were entitled to a proper education and a balanced diet. She convinced thousands of miners to join the UMWA and even influenced their children, who refused to play with others whose fathers didn't join. When the union voted to strike, eight thousand men walked off the job. They set up picket lines outside the mines.

Mine operators vowed to break the union. They advertised for workers willing to cross the picket line. Hicks and the other owners hired guards, passed out guns, and sent men to patrol company boundaries.

Everyone in Black Valley tensed, like soldiers waiting for battle. Fannie didn't flinch. It was rare for a woman to do this kind of work, but she walked the picket lines with the men and rallied strikers to stick it out. She tried to keep peace while the miners and guards heckled one another and often came to blows. During one scuffle, a company guard assaulted Fannie. She pressed charges but lost in court. Luckily, her injuries were not life threatening.

The strike staggered on for weeks, months, nearly a year. Mining families scratched out a living any way they could, with the union providing strike pay from dues paid by members in other parts of the country.

Company guards threatened, thrashed, and sometimes shot striking miners. Miners drummed up guns and shot back. Homemade bombs exploded at the houses of nonunion men and wrecked company buildings and machinery. The sheriff and local judges enforced the law only when it suited the coal companies. Fannie knew the sheriff's deputies doubled as Lewis Hicks's armed thugs.

Hicks's men knew Fannie, too. They didn't want her kind of troublemaker around. Rumors spread that the deputies joked about killing her. Fannie must have wondered if it was time to quit.

All these years, she had believed that if workers stuck together, they'd win a fair share of the money made by their muscle and sweat. The struggle had taken nearly half her life. Her children had grown and had children of their own. Still the fight went on. The courts, local lawmen, and state and national troops all lined up against the union organizers. Maybe her dream was impossible.

FANNIE'S DREAM LIVES ON

BLACK VALLEY, PENNSYLVANIA, 1917

When Lewis Hicks could not hire enough local strikebreakers, he went south, offering jobs to people who didn't know what it was like in the Black Valley. Black sharecroppers, cotton pickers, and miners making even lower wages in Alabama jumped at the chance. They boarded a train in Birmingham, and the guards locked the doors of the cars to keep union organizers from getting to them. Hicks didn't tell the eager-for-work men that he paid low wages. He didn't tell them about the strike. And he didn't tell them that people in the Alle-Kiski Valley might try to kill them for taking their jobs.

Union men bunched together outside the mine. They had heard about the train carrying scabs and were ready to face down the strikebreakers. If they didn't stop these Southerners from working the mines, the strike would fail. The union would be crushed again.

But Fannie had a plan. She waited at a railroad signal outside town where the train would slow and maybe stop. If she could speak to the men on the train, she hoped to convince them to join the union.

Early-1900s Pennsylvania railroad locomotive, similar to the one that Fannie Sellins intersected as it carried strikebreakers to Lewis Hicks's mine in the Alle-Kiski Valley.

She had succeeded in St. Louis. She had succeeded in West Virginia. But the mine operators in Black Valley seemed more dangerous. Men with guns guarded the train whenever it stopped, the same men who had threatened to kill her.

Still, when the train came into view, steam engine hissing, pistons hammering, Fannie picked up her skirts and ran alongside the train cars, shouting at the men inside.

They stared at the woman scrambling over the rugged ground with her hairpins falling out, and opened the windows to hear what she was hollering about. "Don't break the strike!" she called to them. "Support the union."

Could it be true, they wondered? Had they traveled all this way to help bust a union?

"Why else have they locked us in here?" one said.

"That's right. No other reason for it," said another.

More windows came down. Men inside the locked cars pounded on the doors. "We can't get out!"

Fannie shouted, "Workers, unite! Power to the union!"

One man climbed out a train window and dropped to the ground. Those left behind cheered. Up and down the track, men climbed from the windows and jumped to the ground.

Fannie shook the hand of every man who fled the train and then marched with them down the tracks. One hundred men from Alabama crossed a bridge and paraded into town, where union families lined the street, clapping and cheering. If a man wanted to go home, the union gave him a ticket on the next train back. Those workers who wanted to join the strike were welcomed into the union.

The strikers held fast at Hicks's mines, but world events intervened. On April 6, 1917, the United States entered World War I. To support the country's war effort, the striking miners gave up many of their demands and went back to work. Under new wartime regulations, the United States government brokered a wage deal with coal-mine operators across the nation, and Lewis Hicks agreed to give miners a 50 percent pay raise.

The war ended in November 1918, and soon after, the mine operators nixed their end of the

Coal miners' and steel workers' efforts produced war materials like these three-inch shells at a Bethlehem Steel Company factory. To free up men to fight the war, women were trained to manufacture munitions. Bethlehem, Pennsylvania, c. 1918.

contract, in which they had recognized the United Mine Workers Union. Miners in Western Pennsylvania lost what little leverage they had gained and any hope of a new pay increase to cover the spike in prices over the last few years.

By the following summer, Fannie had committed the full force of her personality to buck up the UMWA in Black Valley. In late July 1919, miners walked out at Allegheny Coal & Coke in Brackenridge, Pennsylvania, demanding the company recognize the union. Strikers picketed on public roads near the mine. The sheriff swore in extra deputies, passed out rifles, and sent the men to patrol company boundaries. These were not impartial law enforcement officers. They were thugs and riffraff, deputized at the whim of industrial corporations in the valley.

A tense peace lasted five weeks until an argument broke out between deputies and striking coal miners. On the afternoon of August 26, Fannie arrived in the neighborhood of Abe Roth's grocery shop in Natrona, just a short walk from the mine entrance in Brackenridge. She hoped to convince miners coming off shift to join the strike.

The grocery store was where women gathered to socialize, and children came along hoping for a few pennies for a treat. That muggy summer afternoon, the strikers and deputies exchanged insults, sparking gunfire along the route from the store to the mine. A woman in the crowd suggested that the miners arm themselves for protection.

Fannie disagreed. "We don't want our people carrying," she said. Seven-year-old Stanley F. Rafalko noticed the commotion as he left Abe Roth's store with cigarettes for his father and ran to watch. He saw deputies fire their handguns and between shots, one of them beat retired miner Joseph Starzeleski with a club.

"For God's sake, don't kill him!" Fannie shouted. But they ignored her. One of the deputies aimed at Starzeleski and fired five shots into his back.

Then a man came out of a nearby Allegheny Coal & Coke first-aid shack, carrying an armload of rifles. The man handed them out to the officers

as Fannie continued to rebuke them. One of the deputies aimed a kick at Fannie, and she jumped back, falling to one knee. She struggled toward safety behind the Rafalko family's backyard fence, herding children with her, but the deputy pursued her, swinging his club and hitting Fannie in the head. Then more officers turned on her and fired, hammering her to the ground.

The deputies moved on to attack another worker, not noticing Stanley. His parents and grandpap were calling for him in Polish, but he

ignored them. "I was just a curious kid," he said later.

Stanley ran to Fannie. Despite the blows to her head, Fannie's straw hat remained pinned to her hair. Stanley lifted the brim and saw that she was dead.

Shocked, he ran away, but continued to watch from a distance. The sheriff's officers dragged the bodies to a car, Fannie by her feet and Joseph Starzeleski by his collar, and stacked them into the trunk to haul them away.

That night the justice of the peace charged ten deputies with murder. But the local sheriff's department did not arrest them. Autopsies showed Fannie died of a crushed skull and suffered three gunshots, two to the side of the head and one in her back. Five point-blank gunshots killed Starzeleski. Seven other men were shot but survived.

Three days after Fannie's death, grieving people lined the streets before dawn, waiting for her casket to pass by. Mourners crowded into the little wooden church in New Kensington, where Fannie had lived, a few miles downriver from Natrona.

SAY SLAIN WOMAN LED MOB.

Steel Deputies Testify Organizer Headed Attack on Them.

PITTSBURGH, June 7.—Mrs. Fannie Sellins, organizer for the United Mine Workers, was leading a charging mob of men and women armed with clubs and bricks when she was killed by a volley of shots fired by guards at the plant of the Allegheny Steel Company, according to defense witnesses today at the trial of Edward Mannison and D. J. Riley, Deputy Sheriffs, charged with the murder of the woman union leader. State witnesses had previously testified that there was no disorder at the mine until after the Deputies fired into the crowd.

R. J. Schrandt, a Deputy, testified that after a small group of men had been driven back, Mrs. Sellins organized a mob and led the charge against the line of deputies. Shots were fired from near-by houses, he said, but the guards used their riot sticks until they were broken. Then firing began and when the crowd was dispersed, Mrs. Sellins and Philip Strezelecki, a miner, lay dead on the roadway.

Three men, who said they had been wounded by the Deputies' fire, testified that there had been no attack on the officers and that there was no occasion for shooting.

The *New York Times* reported on the trial of the three men indicted in Fannie Sellins's death. The United Mine Workers of America petitioned for a special prosecutor in an effort to insure an unbiased prosecution, dateline: Pittsburgh, Pennsylvania, June 7, 1923.

In the largest funeral procession in the town's history, thousands paid their respects as Fannie's and Starzeleski's bodies were borne from St. Peter's Catholic Church to the Union Cemetery.

A month later, the Allegheny County coroner's jury convened in Pittsburgh to examine the evidence. The officers who shot Fannie insisted she was leading a riot and that union sympathizers had attacked them with rocks and sticks. The press reported that Fannie Sellins was killed while on picket duty. The jury disregarded the testimony of some sixty eyewitnesses who gave sworn statements that the attack by the deputies was unprovoked.

Form 13—Coroner

CORONER'S JURY VERDICT

State of Pennsylvania,
County of Allegheny. } ss:

Fanny Sellens ___ Deceased

And now, to wit, Sept., 26th, 1919

We, the Jurors empaneled in the above inquisition, do find that

Fanny Sellens
Born ___ 1
abt.
age, 47 years, ___ months, ___ days, ___ Nationality, American
Social relation, Widow ___ Occupation, Labor Organizer, and residing at
5th Ave., and 9th St. New Kensington, Pa.
came to h her death xxx near Allegheny Steel Co. Coal Mine Harrison Twp. Allegheny Co. Pa., on Tuesday, Aug., 26th, 1919 at 4 P. M due to gun shot wound in left temple from gun in the hands or person or persons unknown to the Jury during an attack on the Sheriffs Deputies on Aug., 26th, 1919 .

And from the evidence and Post Mortem examination made the Jury find death was due to the above cause and the same was Justifiable and in self defense and also recommend that Sheriff Haddock be commended in his prompt and successful action on protecting property and persons in that vicinity and the judgement exercised in the selection of his deputies. We also Criticise and deplore the action of Alien or Agitators who instill Anarchy and Bolshevism Doctrines in the minds of UnAmericans and uneducated Aliens.

Portrait of Fannie Sellins, c. 1915.

The jury decided the killings of Fannie and Joseph Starzeleski were justifiable homicide, saying, "There were no innocent bystanders," and "Everyone in the crowd was guilty of rioting."

The crowd of people who witnessed Fannie's death believed she was shot down in cold blood. UMWA leaders fired off telegraphs to President Wilson demanding a federal investigation. One of the deputies accused of shooting Fannie had been heard earlier threatening "to get her." After the shooting, another was heard saying that Fannie Sellins had finally gotten what she deserved.

A Federal Department of Labor investigation languished amid prevailing American fears that labor unions harbored communists. Since the 1917 Bolshevik Revolution in Russia, steel companies had incited this xenophobia and painted strikers as wanting to overthrow the government. This prejudice figured strongly in the attitudes of the coroner's jury that saw union families as a mob of rioters and ruled that the deputies killed Fannie in self-defense.

Under pressure from Fannie's family and the UMWA, a grand jury was called to hear all the evidence. In June 1923, three deputies were indicted for murder and the case went to trial. One of them, the deputy who eyewitnesses claimed shot and killed Fannie, had disappeared. The other two were acquitted of all charges.

Today, both Fannie Sellins's death and her passion for the welfare and rights of working people have been largely forgotten. But her name remains hallowed among union people in Western Pennsylvania, and her spirit lives on whenever someone stands up for the American ideals of equality and justice for all.

Fannie Sellins was buried in Union Cemetery, Arnold, Pennsylvania. The United Mine Workers raised a graveside memorial to Sellins in 1920.

AUTHOR'S NOTE

While researching Fannie Sellins, I was shocked that no one was ever held responsible for her violent killing. This violated my personal sense of justice and, in my opinion, American values. But I soon realized that Fannie's murder was not an isolated instance, and the failure to pursue justice was not unusual at the time. The facts of the case are hardly even remarkable when viewed in the context of the persistent violence perpetrated against American workers for much of our early history.

In this book I've included facts and figures about some of that violence. However, official records of union people like Fannie killed over decades of worker strikes are spotty. No official body count, no reliable numbers of physical assaults, and no definitive records of worker jailings without due process truly document the violence of the struggle for workers' rights. But evidence does exist of a distinct pattern of intimidation and harassment of workers by company-hired gunmen, local law enforcement, and National Guard troops—with little or no redress for the victims. And when this brute force failed to halt strikes, industrial and business owners could often count on the strong arm of the United States Army for assistance, as they did in the Great Railroad Strike of 1877. (See page 36.)

Did workers, too, ever instigate violence in pursuit of their cause? Yes, there are records of union members blatantly attacking company guards and killing scabs. However, this violence was rarely, if ever, officially condoned or orchestrated by the unions, as it was on the part of company owners and managers.

After the shooting of Fannie Sellins, unions across the country used her martyrdom to rally workers in the first nationwide steel strike on September 22, 1919. When 350,000 laborers took to the picket lines in cities such as Lackawanna, New York; Pittsburgh, Pennsylvania; and Pueblo, Colorado, hired gunmen, police, and soldiers lined up against them. Hundreds of workers were intimidated, beaten, hauled from their homes, and jailed on flimsy charges. Federal troops put down the strike in many cities, leading to more violence and several workers' deaths. The combination of anti-immigrant propaganda, armed forces, and a fundamental devaluing of the lives of workers slammed unions into submission. Within ten weeks, the strikers folded. As had happened time and again, they went back to work with no gains, their effort a dismal failure.

Was Fannie Sellins's death, then, in vain? Did her

National Guard soldiers funded by business magnate John D. Rockefeller's Colorado Fuel and Iron Company aim machine guns at a tent camp, temporary home to 1,200 union families. Pelting the tents with rifle and machine-gun fire, they kill an eleven-year-old boy. After a fourteen-hour siege, the soldiers burn the camp. Nineteen people die, including two women and eleven children trapped beneath their tent. Ludlow, Colorado, 1914.

courage and belief in the rights of workers accomplish nothing?

Hardly. True, the lengths to which powerful corporations have been willing to go to protect their profits highlights an unbroken trail of shame running through our nation's history. And changing those conditions required many, many sacrifices like Fannie's over a long time—more than a century.

The power of law—President Franklin D. Roosevelt's labor-friendly New Deal and the U.S. Congress's 1935 National Labor Relations Act (also known as the Wagner Act)—finally compelled business and industry to pay attention to workers' grievances.

It was ordinary people who wanted change and demanded it. Ordinary people, such as Fannie Sellins, with hope and vision made sacrifices so that all of us might receive benefits such as workplace safety, the five-day workweek, the eight-hour workday, sick pay, and paid vacation time. Though these ordinary, everyday, hardworking people might not be recorded in history books, they strove to create the change America needed.

After workers made gains in the mid-twentieth century, American labor unions lost strength. Today, opponents debate the need for a minimum wage and workers' right to organize. Many companies cut health benefits and retirement. The gap between the rich and the poor stretches as wide as it did in Fannie's lifetime. At the time this book went to print, thirteen million American children were living in poverty, some half million of whom labor in the fields that grow America's food.

Poor workers thirst for hope. They hunger for the kind of leadership Fannie Sellins modeled. When I started researching her story, I had one question: How did she have the courage to stand up for the working poor against such huge and deadly odds? Her death in 1919 is well documented in public records, photographs, witness accounts, and newspaper articles. The United States census records Fannie's birth in Cincinnati, Ohio, in 1872. But between those two notable dates are few details. I found no living family members, and as is true for much of history, there exists little written record of poor people's lives.

Fannie told union miners in Illinois in 1919 that she had "known nothing but a sewing machine for fifteen years." Census records from April 1910 note that she lived in a rental house in St. Louis, Missouri, with three of her children: John (age seventeen), Josephine (age fourteen), and Julia (age twelve). It seems that her oldest daughter had, by then, left home. Fannie reported that her younger daughters attended school that year, that she was a widow and mother of four, and that she worked as a seamstress.

History did not record precisely what Fannie said to her fellow seamstresses to convince them to organize and join Ladies' Local 67 of the United Garment Workers of America. Likewise, there is no hard evidence of how discouraged she might have felt when facing powerful mine owners, such as Lewis Hicks, or of exactly what she shouted to the men on the train from Birmingham, Alabama, in February 1917. In these instances, I believe that her actions speak even louder than whatever words she might have said, so I have filled in some cracks in the research with my own phrasings. Still, I believe that this book as a whole truthfully portrays Fannie Sellins's life and her commitment to working people. And in writing it, I discovered that many people shared the same courage she demonstrated. They may not be remembered individually like Fannie, but throughout history many ordinary people had the courage to risk their lives to fight a system they believed was unjust.

They did not look away from the problems in their neighborhoods, communities, and workplaces. Like Fannie, they tackled them head-on. Today, we still need leaders with Fannie's courage, commitment, and compassion, leaders who will not flinch but will keep dreaming of and working toward fairness for all. Maybe each of us carries the capacity to demonstrate those qualities in some way that will make a difference.

GLOSSARY

arbitration (*noun*): In reference to labor strikes, *arbitration* is the process by which workers and company management each submit their side of a dispute to a neutral third party. Both agree to abide by the compromise decided by the neutral person or group, the *arbitrator*.

boycott (*verb*): To stop buying or using the goods or services of a certain company or country as a protest; the noun *boycott* is the protest itself.

collective bargaining (*noun*): The process by which wages, hours, rules, and working conditions are negotiated and agreed upon by an employer and a labor union.

Great Depression (*noun*): The economic crisis beginning with the stock market crash in 1929 and continuing through the 1930s.

lockout (*noun*): A situation in which an employer shuts down a workplace during a labor dispute, suspends operations, or does not allow workers to return to their jobs until they agree to certain wages, terms, or conditions of employment.

militia (*noun*): A body of citizens enrolled for military service, and called on periodically for drills but serving full time only in emergencies.

National Guard (*noun*): As originally drafted, the United States Constitution recognized existing state militias, and gave them power to. "execute the Laws of the Union, suppress Insurrections and repel Invasion" (Article I, Section 8, Clause 15). The traditional state militias were redefined and recreated as the National Guard, via the Militia Act of 1903.

organize (*verb*): In reference to labor unions, the act of convincing workers to join the union or to support a strike.

picket (*verb*): To stand or walk outside a business or industry, often carrying protest signs, in an attempt to dissuade or prevent workers or customers from entering the establishment during a strike.

picket line (*noun*): A row or rows formed by union members or sympathizers in front of or surrounding a factory, store, mine, etc., during a strike.

scab (*noun*): A worker who refuses to take part in a strike and takes a striking worker's place on the job.

strike (*noun*): A work stoppage by workers in a united front in protest of the unfair wages or unsafe working conditions imposed by an employer and/or to compel the employer to meet their demands.

sweatshop (*noun*): A factory where workers do piecework for poor pay and are prevented from forming unions; common in the clothing industry.

union (*noun*): A number of persons, states, etc., joined by a common purpose; in the case of labor or trade unions, workers unite to gain power to bargain for better pay, working conditions, or other benefits.

xenophobia (*noun*): A fear or hatred of people from different countries or cultures.

TIME LINE OF SELECT EVENTS IN THE AMERICAN LABOR STRUGGLE, 1877–1935

Time lines of labor-union victories do not always show the depth of the struggles and the sacrifices made to achieve gains in workers' rights. A link to a traditional labor-union time line is located on page 42 of this book. However, this time line shows valiant efforts by union workers that were crushed by industrial corporations with the backing of local, state, and/or the federal government. After each instance, union people eventually found the wherewithal to rally and try again, until 1934, when companies were forced by the federal government to recognize unions and negotiate with workers. The United Garment Workers Strike in St. Louis, which Fannie helped organize, is included, though it is a notable exception. That strike was a clear victory for laborers.

1877 THE GREAT NATIONWIDE RAILROAD STRIKE, BALTIMORE, MARYLAND

⚙ The Maryland National Guard fought its way through striking railroad workers in Baltimore on July 20. The strike against wage cuts swept west along the rails through Chicago, Kansas City, Pittsburgh, St. Louis, to San Francisco—100,000 workers halting commerce for forty-five days. President Rutherford B. Hayes sent federal troops to end the strike, and workers went back to their jobs, taking lower wages. This set a precedent for using federal soldiers to enforce corporate interests against labor.

1886 HAYMARKET SQUARE, CHICAGO, ILLINOIS

⚙ During a rally on May 4 to support workers seeking an eight-hour workday, a pipe bomb exploded in Chicago's Haymarket Square, panicking both the demonstrators and the police, who opened fire. Seven policemen and at least four civilians died, and more than sixty demonstrators were hurt. In a frenzy, local police rounded up labor leaders and suspected radicals, plus hundreds of workers. No evidence ever identified who threw the bomb, but eight men stood trial, and four were hanged. Historians still debate the accuracy of the charges against these men and the fairness of the trial.

1892 THE HOMESTEAD LOCKOUT, NEAR PITTSBURGH, PENNSYLVANIA

⚙ In one of the most serious disputes in U.S. labor history, after days of demonstrating, members of the Amalgamated Association of Iron and Steel Workers faced off at the Carnegie Steel Company against company-hired agents from the Pinkerton National Detective Agency in a fourteen-hour skirmish. After collective bargaining failed, Carnegie shut down its Homestead plant and locked out the union workers. Angered at losing their jobs, the laborers took over the plant. After several people died in skirmishes, nine workers among them, state militia arrived, armed with Winchester rifles and Gatling machine guns. They forced the workers to back down and sidelined the union in Western Pennsylvania for two generations.

1903–1904 Colorado Labor Wars

⚙ Striking miners were arrested and forced to leave Colorado after mine owners secretly financed vigilantes (self-appointed law enforcers) and National Guard soldiers to crush the miners' union. Seventy-two percent of Colorado voters had approved an eight-hour workday, but the mine owners ignored them and paid Pinkerton detectives to incite violence and blame it on the strikers. When dynamite exploded at a railroad depot, killing thirteen and injuring six nonunion men, the Mine Owners Association seized control of the investigation by threatening to lynch the county sheriff—a union member who had been elected by the people and didn't favor company interests. Laborers in the Cripple Creek mining district would not organize and win their rights for another generation.

1909–1911 United Garment Workers Strike Marx & Haas, St. Louis, Missouri

⚙ After negotiations for better pay and working conditions broke down, the Marx & Haas Clothing Company locked out one thousand workers, including United Garment Workers of America Ladies' Local 67, of which Fannie Sellins was president. Union members picketed the factory until they were prohibited from doing so by a judge. Still, the strikers held out for two years, while a national boycott of Marx & Haas Clothing pressured the company to sign a contract with the union for improved pay and working conditions.

1913–1914 United Mine Workers Strike, Colliers, West Virginia

⚙ September 13, 1913, United Mine Workers of America (UMWA) went on strike against the West Virginia–Pittsburgh Coal Company, which continued operations with nonunion labor. The company won a court injunction to prohibit the UMWA from organizing local workers. Union leaders, including Fannie Sellins, were jailed for speaking at public rallies. The strike settled in June 1914, with workers re-hired at slightly better wages and working conditions but dissolution of the UMWA in the region.

1914 Ludlow Massacre, Ludlow, Colorado

⚙ On April 20, Colorado National Guard soldiers aimed a machine gun at a union camp during a strike in Southern Colorado. Company gunmen harassed strikers, shot at them from an armored car and beamed searchlights on their tents at night. The miners thought the Guard had arrived to protect them from dangerous harassment by the camp guards, but the soldiers and guards destroyed two tent camps, burning one to the ground and killing two women and eleven children. The massacre brought criticism to principal owner John D. Rockefeller and highlighted the Colorado miners' grievances, but little improved for them.

What remains of a striking coal miners' tent colony after attack and burning by National Guard troops. Ludlow, Colorado, 1914.

1919 United Mine Workers Strike Allegheny Coal & Coke, Brackenridge, Pennsylvania

⚙ After Fannie's death, the United Mine Workers of America (UMWA) continued its labor action against the Allegheny Coal & Coke Company. The next month the American Federation of Labor (AFL) struck the United States Steel Corporation with the same demands—higher wages, an eight-hour workday, and recognition of unions. The strike spread across the nation, and eventually 350,000 workers walked out. But companies whipped up prejudice against unions, painting workers as communists, and strikers lost public support. Federal and state soldiers ended the strike, and UMWA and AFL workers returned to their jobs with no gains.

1920–1921 West Virginia Coal Wars and Battle of Blair Mountain

⚙ West Virginia miners lived in nearly feudal conditions—their homes, schools, churches, stores, and even their politicians owned by the mine bosses. When the miners went on strike, coal operators hired gunmen, including sheriff's deputies, to assault, arrest, and blacklist workers and evict their families from their homes. When two union sympathizers were shot on the steps of the county courthouse, five thousand union miners armed themselves to face the corporate gunmen and soldiers. When the federal government sent ground troops, and bomber planes landed at a nearby airfield, the strikers surrendered.

1934 West Coast Longshoremen Strike

⚙ In what is also known as the West Coast Waterfront Strike, longshoremen (dockworkers) closed ports in California, Oregon, and Washington for eighty-three days, demanding union recognition and hiring halls run by unions, not bosses. Two strikers were shot dead and more than one hundred wounded by police on a sidewalk in San Francisco on July 5. The police killings triggered a four-day general strike, and sailors and workers throughout the city joined the shutdown. Employers eventually agreed to government arbitration to end the strike. The longshoremen's victory launched the modern labor movement in the western United States, in which workers have the right by law to form unions and bargain with employers.

Policeman wielding a nightstick engages with a striker during the citywide general strike. San Francisco, California, 1934.

1934 Black Friday, Minneapolis Truckers Strike

⚙ After truckers striking for improved wages and better working conditions nearly shut down commercial transportation in the upper Midwest, Minneapolis police fired on crowds of strikers at the city's central market, killing two and wounding more than sixty. Political pressure from President Franklin D. Roosevelt averted all-out warfare in the streets. Companies needing the administration's help to finance their credit agreed to sit down and talk with strikers and accept government help in reaching an agreement. Thus the International Brotherhood of Teamsters was born.

1934 AUTO-LITE STRIKE, TOLEDO, OHIO

⚙ In what is also known as the "Battle of Toledo," sheriff's deputies used tear gas and fire hoses against Electric Auto-Lite Company strikers. The city's 80 percent unemployment rate, a result of the Great Depression, had led factory managers to reduce wages and inspired thousands of citizens to support the strikers. National Guard troops provoked a five-day battle in the streets. People fought with fists and bricks; soldiers fired on the crowd, killing two and injuring more than two hundred. Forty thousand citizens threat-

ened to shut down the city. Electric Auto-Lite finally gave in and signed the first contract with what would become the United Auto Workers.

1934 NATIONAL TEXTILE WORKERS STRIKE, NEWNAN, GEORGIA

⚙ Charged with picketing for better hours and working conditions at a cotton mill in Newnan, Georgia, sixteen women and one hundred and twelve men were imprisoned. A Labor Day textile workers' strike in North Carolina quickly spread across the South and up the Eastern Seaboard. Soon, nearly half a million workers joined the strike. Company guards and Georgia National Guard troops were dispatched in at least seven states, smashing the strike in three weeks. Penniless workers, faced with brutal violence, started returning to their jobs, but companies refused to re-hire 72,000 strikers. Unions remain weak in the South to the present day.

1935 NATIONAL LABOR RELATIONS ACT

⚙ The presidential election of 1932 sparked a major turning point for American labor unions, bring-

The Georgia National Guard rounds up strikers gathered outside the Newnan Textile Mill. Newnan, Georgia, 1934.

ing pro-labor president Franklin D. Roosevelt into office in 1933, along with a Congress sympathetic to labor. The National Labor Relations Act, also known as the Wagner Act, guaranteed workers the right to form unions and collectively bargain for fair wages and workplace safety. The law formed the National Labor Relations Board to protect both employers' and employees' rights and to intervene when labor and management disputes become deadlocked.

NOTES

Page 1: Stanley Rafalko, The Fannie Sellins Project interview, November 16, 1985, transcript (Pennsylvania State University Library, University Park, PA), p. 2.

Page 2: "Faster!" Rose Feurer, ed., "Washington Avenue Garment District." *The St. Louis Labor History Tour* (St. Louis, MO: St. Louis Bread and Roses, Inc., 1994), p. 9.

Page 2: "You bleed on the fabric, you pay for it." Scott, Miriam Finn, "The Spirit of the Girl Strikers," *The Outlook*, Vol. 94, February 1910, p. 393.

Page 4: "All the doors . . . fire should come." "Two Women Fighting Sweatshop System to Help Save Bodies and Souls of Children," *The Tacoma Times*, October 16, 1911, p. 5.

Page 7: "Not fair . . . scabs!" Feurer, Associate Professor, Northern Illinois University, DeKalb, IL, author phone interview, October 8, 2007.

Page 8: "Help us fight . . . die in the mines . . . in our daily work." Proceedings of the Twenty-Third Annual Convention of the United Mine Workers of America, January 16–February 2, 1912, Vol. One (Indianapolis, IN: The Cheltenham-Aetna Press, 1912), p. 624. Retrieved from http://www.books.google.com.

Page 10: "Injury to one is an injury to all." Feurer, e-mail to author, *Theatrical Rendition of Fannie Sellins's Speeches During Marx & Haas Strike 1909–1910*, St. Louis, MO, December 21, 2013.

Page 10: "Pass the hat." James Cassedy, "A Bond of Sympathy: The Life and Tragic Death of Fannie Sellins," *Labor's Heritage*, Vol. 4, No. 4., Winter 1992, p. 36.

Page 14: "in their homes or on the street." Richard D. Lunt, *Law and Order vs. the Miners: West Virginia, 1907–1933* (Hamden, CT: Archon Books, 1979), p. 20.

Page 15: "I am free . . . obey the law." "Mass Meeting in Wellsburg," *The Wheeling Majority* (Wheeling, WV, December 1913), p. 1.

Page 16: "I do not advise . . . last resort." *Application for Clemency*. Case File 28-684. U.S. Pardon Attorney, November 22, 1916.

Page 26: "We don't want our people carrying." Richard Gazarik, *Black Valley: The Life & Death of Fannie Sellins* (Latrobe, PA: Saint Vincent College, 2014), p. 60.

Page 26: "For God's sake, don't kill him!" Ron E. Roberts, Carol Cook-Roberts, *Mother Jones and Her Sisters: A Century of Women Activists in the American Coal Fields* (Dubuque, IA: Kendall/Hunt Publishing Company, 1993), p. 64.

Page 30: "There were no innocent . . . guilty of rioting." Meyerhuber, p. 55.

Page 30: "to get her." Meyerhuber, p. 54.

Page 34: "known nothing but a sewing machine for fifteen years." Proceedings of the Twenty-Third Annual Convention of the United Mine Workers of America, p. 622.

SOURCES

Cassedy, James. "A Bond of Sympathy: The Life and Tragic Death of Fannie Sellins." *Labor's Heritage*, Vol. 4, No. 4. Winter (1992).

"Fannie Sellins Dies on Battlefield of Labor." *St. Louis Labor*, August 30, 1919.

"Fatal Mine Riot Inquest Held Today." *Pittsburgh Leader*, September 26, 1919.

Ferrandiz, Susan. E-mail to author. January 8, 2014. *Application for Clemency*. Case File 28-684. U.S. Pardon Attorney, November 22, 1916.

Feurer, Rosemary, ed. "Washington Avenue Garment District." *St. Louis Labor History Tour*. St. Louis, MO: St. Louis Bread and Roses, Inc., 1994.

Feurer, Rosemary, Associate Professor, Northern Illinois University, DeKalb, IL, author phone interview, October 8, 2007.

Feurer, Rosemary. E-mail to author. *Theatrical Rendition of Fannie Sellins's Speeches During Marx & Haas Strike 1909–1910*, St. Louis, MO, December 21, 2013.

Gazarik, Richard. *Black Valley: The Life & Death of Fannie Sellins*. Latrobe, PA : Saint Vincent College, 2014.

Hilton, W. B. Ohio Valley Trades and Labor Assembly, letter to Mr. James A. Finch, U.S. Department of Justice, Washington, D.C., July 7, 1914.

"In Contempt of Dayton's Court." *Wheeling Majority*. Wheeling, WV, December 1913.

Lunt, Richard D. *Law and Order vs. the Miners: West Virginia, 1907–1933*. Hamden, CT: Archon Books, 1979.

"Man and Woman Shot: Mrs. Fannie Sellins Killed," *Valley Daily News*, Tarentum, PA, August 27, 1919.

Marx & Haas Clothing Corp. versus Union Local 26 of the UGWA, et al. Circuit Court, City of St. Louis, December Term 1909, Case 60718.

"Mass Meeting in Wellsburg," *Wheeling Majority*, Wheeling, WV, December 1913.

Meyerhuber, Carl I. *Less Than Forever: The Rise and Decline of Union Solidarity in Western Pennsylvania, 1914–1948*. Selinsgrove, PA: Susquehanna University Press, London and New York: Associated University Presses, 1987.

Meyerhuber, Carl I. "The Alle-Kiski Valley Coal Wars, 1913–1919," *Western Pennsylvania Historical Magazine*, Vol. 63, No. 3, 1980.

Murray, Philip, President, District 5, United Mine Workers of America, Pittsburgh, PA. Western Union Telegram to John L. Lewis, August 27, 1919, photocopy, Pennsylvania State University Library, University Park, PA.

Proceedings of the Twenty-Third Annual Convention of the United Mine Workers of America, January 16–February 2, 1912. Vol. One, Indianapolis, IN: The Cheltenham-Aetna Press, 1912.

Rafalko, Stanley. The Fannie Sellins Project interview, November 16, 1985, transcript, Pennsylvania State University Library, University Park, PA.

Roberts, Ron E., Carol Cook-Roberts, *Mother Jones and Her Sisters: A Century of Women Activists in the American Coal Fields*. Dubuque, IA: Kendall/Hunt Publishing Company, 1993.

"Say Slain Woman Led Mob: Steel Deputies Testify Organizer Headed Attack on Them," *New York Times*, June 8, 1925.

Scott, Miriam Finn, "The Spirit of the Girl Strikers," *The Outlook*, Vol. 94, February 1910, p. 393.

Slomkoski, Anthony, United Steel Workers of America #1196, Retired. Brackenridge, PA, author interview, July 24, 2010.

"Steel Mill Men Warn Judge Gary." *Pittsburgh Daily Dispatch*, August 27, 1919.

"Steel Trust's Hellish Crew Desecrates Head," *New Majority*, September 20, 1919.

"Two Women Fighting Sweatshop System to Help Save Bodies and Souls of Children," *Tacoma Times*, October 16, 1911.

Wolman, Leo, Paul Wander, Paul, H. K. Herwitz, and

Eleanor Mack. *The Clothing Workers of Chicago, 1910–1922.* Chicago Joint Board, Amalgamated Clothing Workers of America, 1922.

Yost, L. N., M.D., Jail Physician, Marion County Jail. Letter To Whom It May Concern: United States Department of Justice, Washington D.C., June 12, 1914.

WEBSITES FOR MORE INFORMATION

- -

The History Channel: www.history.com/topics/labor

Illinois Labor Historical Society: www.illinoislaborhistory.org/articles/169-fannie-sellins.html

Labor Heritage Foundation: www.laborheritage.org

Labor History Timeline 1642-2011, Western States Center: http://www.roadmapproject.org/wp-content/uploads/2013/08/Timeline-of-Labor-History1.pdf

The National Women's History Museum: www.nwhm.org/online-exhibits/progressiveera/introprogressive.html

University of Pittsburgh Labor Legacy: www.library.pitt.edu/labor_legacy/Sellins.html

Women in Labor History Time Line: www.afscme.org/for-members/womens-leadership-training/leadership-tools/body/Women_in_Labor_History_Timeline.pdf

BOOKS FOR FURTHER READING

- -

Note: An asterisk denotes books written for adults.

NONFICTION

Bartoletti, Susan Campbell. *Kids on Strike!* New York: HMH Books for Young Readers, 2008.

Berlatsky, Noah, ed. *Are Unions Still Relevant?* (At Issue series), San Diego, CA: Greenhaven Press, 2013.

Brown, Monica. *Side by Side/Lado a Lado: The Story of Dolores Huerta and Cesar Chavez/La Historia de Dolores Huerta y Cesar Chavez*, Bilingual edition, New York: Rayo, 2010.

*Dray, Philip. *There Is Power in a Union: The Epic Story of Labor in America.* New York: Doubleday, 2010.

Miller, Connie Colwell. *Mother Jones: Labor Leader* (Graphic Biography series). North Mankato, MN: Capstone Press, 2007.

Nelson, S. D. *Digging a Hole to Heaven: Coal Miner Boys.* New York: Abrams Books for Young Readers, 2014.

Skurzynski, Gloria. *Sweat and Blood: A History of U.S. Labor Unions* (People's History series). Minneapolis, MN: Lerner Publishing Group, 2008.

Warren, Sarah and Robert Casilla. *Dolores Huerta: A Hero to Migrant Workers.* Seattle, WA: Two Lions, 2012.

FICTION

Farrell, Mary Cronk. *Fire in the Hole!* Boston: Clarion Books, 2004.

Lieurance, Suzanne. *The Locket: Surviving the Triangle Shirtwaist Fire* (Historical Fiction Adventures series). New York: Enslow Publishers, Inc., 2008.

Lyon, George Ella and Christopher Cardinale. *Which Side Are You On?: The Story of a Song*. El Paso, TX: Cinco Puntos Press, 2011.

Paterson, Katherine. *Bread and Roses, Too*. Boston: Clarion Books, 2006.

Winthrop, Elizabeth. *Counting on Grace*. New York: Wendy Lamb Books, 2006.

ACKNOWLEDGMENTS

I'm intensely grateful to my agent, Stephen Fraser, and my editor, Howard Reeves, for believing in Fannie's story, and to Maria Middleton, Michael Clark, Orlando Dos Reis, and Kathy Lovisolo, who helped make it such a powerful book and get it into the hands of young readers. I am greatly indebted to members of my writing group, who read many versions of *Fannie Never Flinched* and lent encouragement and support through the years: Mary Douthitt, Claire Rudolf Murphy, Meghan Nuttall Sayres, and Lynn Caruso, and also Beth Cooley and Kris Dinnison, who helped in the homestretch. I received a huge boost of confidence and research funding from the Society of Children's Book Writers and Illustrators, which awarded this project the 2008 Nonfiction Work-in-Progress Award endowed by James Cross Giblin.

Many people helped me with my research, and without them I never could have written this book. I am especially grateful to Anthony Slomkoski, a retired steelworker who gave me a tour of the area where Fannie Sellins was shot and shared his collection of historical documents. I also owe much to the generosity of James Cassedy, Rosemary Feurer, and Susan Ferrandiz.

Other people and institutions to which I am so grateful: author Philip Dray; James Green (Professor of History, University of Massachusetts Boston); Robert Anthony Bruno (Professor of Labor Studies, University of Illinois); Joseph A. McCartin (Professor of U.S. Labor, Social and Political History, Georgetown University); University of Pittsburgh Labor Legacy Web Site and Archives Service Center; Mike Matejka (Illinois Labor History Society); Elise Bryant (Acting Executive Director, Labor Heritage Foundation); Laura Bell (Photographs Manager at the West Virginia and Regional History Center); Zach Brodt (Records Manager, University of Pittsburgh); Miriam Meislik (Media Curator, University of Pittsburgh); Jim Quigel (Historical Collections and Labor Archives, Paterno Library, Pennsylvania State University); Alexandra Bainbridge (Special Collections, Pennsylvania State University Libraries); Timothy Babcock; Laura Elizabeth Pinsent (Pennsylvania State University Libraries Special Collections); Anne Evenhaugen (Reference Librarian, Smithsonian American Art Museum/National Portrait Gallery Library); Holly Reed (Archives Specialist, Still Pictures Reference, National Archives); Jaime Bourassa (Missouri History Museum); Sumi Shadduck and Gillian Sayre (Spokane Public Library); and Robin Lightly (coalmininghistorypa.org).

I'm grateful to the Catholic Community of St. Ann, Spokane, Washington, for nurturing women's gifts, calling them forth, and supporting them and me during the gestating years of this book. Always grateful for the love and support of my family and friends, Mom and Dad (Iron Workers Union Local #505), Mike, Brandon, Clarice, Monica, and Dylan.

INDEX